doing

Cid Corman

nothing doing

a new directions book

Book and cover design by Erik Rieselbach
Manufactured in the United States of America
New Directions Books are printed on acid-free paper.
First published as a New Directions Paperbook
    Original in 1999
Published simultaneously in Canada by Penguin Books
    Canada Limited

Library of Congress Cataloging-in-Publication Data
Corman, Cid.
Nothing doing / Cid Corman.
    p.   cm.
"A New Directions paperbook original" – T.p. verso.
ISBN 0-8112-1425-7 (alk. paper)
I. Title.
PS3553.065N67   1999
811'.54–dc21   99-31894
                                                    CIP

New Directions Books are published for James Laughlin
by New Directions Publishing Corporation,
80 Eighth Avenue, New York 10011

poems from
the 80s and 90s

for
Peggy
and
Griselda

*for
holding
the fort*

psalm
xxiv

The earth and
the fulness
thereof. Lift

up your heads –
O ye gates –
for as long

as is – and
the glory
shall enter.

psalm
xxv

No way no
judgment but
mother – dad –

let me be
child of you
children – to

be cared for
and care for –
unredeemed.

**psalm
xliii**

Come
to the hills
and in their

shadow and
light feel well
come.

metaballon
anapauetai

They call it life
but it means death –
human bias

the sound of a
string – released is
regathering.

Though you say you'll come
more often than not you don't –
since you say and don't
you won't be expected to
unless you say that you won't.

the
principle

: so was I at this new-seen vision:
    wanted to see how the image com-
    bined with the circle and settled in;
but my own powers were not enough:
    unless my mind were to be stricken
    by some brilliance informing its will.
Imagination here lacked the strength;
    but now my desire and wish turned round,
    just as a wheel similarly's moved,
the love that moves the sun and other stars.

admiral

Arms unknown to them

nor are they fitted
for arms – well-built but

timid and fearful

facing heaven-sent
conquering minions

of a Christian God.

**praise
from
ripley**

BELIEVE IT OR NOT
the most outstanding
poet of all time

(Parma Italy)
F. M. Grapaldo
1464

to 1515
able to compose
a pair of poems

in Latin writing
simultaneous-
ly ONE WITH EACH HAND!

**sir
:damnable proud**

Tall handsome bold – high
forehead – long-faced – a
kind of pig-eye. First

that brought Tobacco
into England and
into fashion. Small

voice – broad Devonshire.
He loved a wench well.
Carlo Buffono.

King James couldnt help
saying – Mon – I have
heard rawly of thee.

Pear being pared ah

the sweetness of the drops on

the edge quite enough

Hard going way worn

dreaming of waste after waste

going on and on

A dewdrop world ay

a dewdrop world but even

so – but even so

Just resting –
letting the
breezes make
something of
a body.

**so
easily**

Wind sweeping
the willow
and willow

the wind but
neither can
be brushed off.

Going on this way

from one day to the next and

getting no better

now all by myself wonder

if there's any where to go

With the birds singing

on every mountainside

flowers blossoming

the spring in every heart

there isnt the space for me!

If you would step into the infinite –

Only go into the finite everywhere.

1848

I can sympathize
with the barberry
whose business is

only to ripen
its fruit (tho maybe
not sweeten it)

protect it with thorns
so all winter it
holds on unless

hungry crows come to
pluck it. I mean
merely spend words

enough to purchase
silence with – tho few
poets prize it.

O Venus – here I

am so much hung meat...

God! Give me the pluck

to think there's more yet!

**moody
mary**

Not a prospect but

is dark on earth – as
to knowledge and joy

from externals but

the prospect of a
dying bed reflects

luster on the rest.

babbalanja

Giants are

in our germs
but we are

dwarfs stagger-

ing under
heads over-

grown. Heaped our

measures burst.

We die of
too much life.

**after
"amen!"**

This "all" feeling, though –

there is some truth in.
You mustve felt it

lying on the grass

on a summer's day.
Your legs send out shoots –

your hair feels like leaves.

**the
cancelled
close**

Here ends a story

not unwarranted by what

sometimes happens in

this incomprehensible

world of ours – hoist and belay.

22nd january
1869

Twenty Hill Hollow

Chee chool cheedildy

choodildy – meadow

lark – Queed-lix boodle –

sweet as the sky gave.

**late
autumn**

Your little Note dropped
in upon us as
softly as the Snow

followed – as spacious
and as stainless – a
paragraph – perhaps –

from Every Where –
to which we never
go – We miss you more

this time – I think – than
all the time before.
Emily – with Love.

nces

I had a sense of

my preparedness
only a person

lost in pursuing

a calling loved knows.
As natural as

breathing. All of life.

**candle
light**

Murasaki sashimi

tsukemono in tiny
white dishes minimal light

and maximum shadow with

kamaboko tofu and
miso black lacquer lid lifts

behold with steam white *gohan!*

**for
the
end
of
it**

Character

to quit when
you're losing

and now all

they had was
the habit

to endure

butterfly

your butterfly of legend
papa

came along to find you on the beach
and drank from your glass
a swig of sweet wine

and then went off
bumbling about
like any old
sot

ruth

We think of
you often
in Portland –

One night there
Mark & I
walked around

a small pond –
raindrops made
ripples. At

that moment
I said to
Mark – Somehow

this makes me
think of Cid –
and he smiled

and said he'd
been thinking
of you too.

**ask
theseus**

Is this what I mean?
Is this what means me?
Am I what this means?

Meaning loses us.
We are lost within
whatever we find.

Jesus put in his

thirty-three years and
was charged for it. And

how many years have

you been at it? What
moment do you think

delighted him most?

Jalal-ud-Din – dont

you get it yet? Poetry's

the divinity.

alighieri

To have gone

through this hell
and to find

it all in

the end a
poem a

comedy.

the
interest

There was a time when
Michelangelo
wanted the marble

to be real people –
a form of pity.
Slowly rock learned him

better and he turned
more and more to it
to lend them its life.

**the
route**

Dont read Shakespeare – let

Shakespeare speak within you the

words from which he came.

**the
lady**

She was always

at flood – came with
it and went – an

island – John Donne –

an island – a
woman we are

still waiting on.

**tout
d'un
cuyp**

Cows long before now
on a hillside on
a ridge adjoining

the sea and a maid
a-milking. All shape
and color. Sort of

a ceremony –
as unlike what it
is as it depicts.

orbit

We are the mirrors
of Rembrandt's portraits
of himself. But he –

who painted and paints
us yet – knew we were –
even as we are –

more than mirrors – more
than surfaces re-
flecting surfaces –

we were to meet at
this painted point. Look
at us reading here.

das
kapital

Marx's error one
the Brothers didnt
make. They knew you can't

sit down and program
a community
but only grow by

giving yourself all
altogether to it
and getting the joke.

40

riverrun

Joyce understood how

the first word always
hankers after the

last confirming it

reverberating –
as if nothing else

could be said enough.

**a
rose
for
gertrude**

Graved within

big and black

laid out flat

smooth stone: STEIN.

beyond
crit

Beckett knew life is

not absurd – but mad
and contagiously

so and must be faced

even as posed on
its own stage – potty –

indulging language.

**the
word**

Death is "wonderful"

as Charles dying felt
reiterating

beyond all vision

the truth of the act
of being for a

moment a moment!

44

**for
rené**

A lover
to the end –
the passion

of life to
be alive
beyond all

destiny –
be come to
this moment.

samperi

Frank – your mother died

when you were only a babe

in her arms and yet

you – until the day you died –

felt those arms holding you still.

devotion

Alone as Mother

Teresa mustve been in

trying to forget

she was in helping others

to remember it for her.

**riva
san
vitale**

Death always

reminding
us – a breath

is a breath.

The soul and
spirit of

a poet.

islands

They discovered the

world searching for what might make

eating interesting.

Socrates

clearly could
neither read

nor write but

could walk and
talk – fuck – and

drink hemlock.

All I had

to say to
you – brother –

was only

and always –
even as

now – brother.

He needed

her to fill
the hole in

his head with

a wisp of
a smile – feel

da Vinci.

conte
crayon

Seeing Leonardo's face
as he drew it – saw it – knew
it – about 1512 – red

chalk – Raphael's Plato – not
altogether him perhaps –
red paper – line become flesh –

whose hair had grown thin too but
flowed over – foaming eyebrows –
into an uncut beard – nose

decisive – mouth stubborn – eyes
those of a half-blind eagle
fixed on an eternal mouse.

They find in the ancient tomb
recently uncovered a
crown of countless pendants like those

Kudara commonly wore
and I think suddenly of
night glittering overhead.

People like Rembrandt
make my day. He looks
at me with a faint

smile – without pity
and without contempt.
He knows what I know

and knows I know. Do
you know what it means
just to have a friend?

**seeing
paint**

The brash swash

and blaze of
the golden

sash bulking

body to
sit enthroned

with a face!

Painting the music
Vermeer – harpsichord –
"virginal" in mind?

the sound imagined –
the latest silence –
coloring echoes

and all that light so
refined by space it
sings like crinoline.

**the
art
of
nature**

Arp dropt his little
sculptures in the Bois
but the child has found

and comes running to
bestow on me – hand
at hand – an acorn.

**a
few
years
yet**

The patience of the
more than a hundred
year old sculptor met

was letting a chunk
of great wood ripen
in his atelier

before finding the
figure he was to
elicit from it.

the
exercise

Shizumi

from the height
of the nuns'

temple steps

running down
as the sun

sets to me.

3

Who were we to die?

Who are we to live?

I want the words
so simple and
true you think they

have come out of
your own mouth and
are breathing you.

In a moment
all one cherishes
vanishes

Which dream is
the dream – the one
we awaken from

and go into or
from which we
never emerge?

I will tell you the secret.
Listen.

      What is it? – you ask?

I keep telling you:

      Listen.

efficacies

I pray for the sun
and the sun rises –
I pray for the night

and the night falls. I
pray for you and here
you are! What more – pray?

If these words be ours
and the words nothing –
as they are – then we

are nothing too. Yes –
yes – let it be so.
But let the words know.

I'm shitting
alone – at home.
Naturally

the telephone
rings and rings and
rings – wont wipe

it: first things first.
Which takes as
long as it takes.

**the
posthumous**

I wouldve like her
to have known others
finally have come

to find her poems
and love them – love her.
We like to believe

it doesnt matter
to the dead one way
or the other and

it doesnt. But I
know. And I know she
wouldve savored this.

You want to know

what you did wrong
to have deserved

such a fate. Mom –

you've brought us here
and led us on

to wonder too.

Is it every

leaf silently crying I

I I am the tree?

Why should I
think of her
now? But then

she was my
mother. She
thought of me.

And if you
had never
been? Am I

speaking to
an ant or
Jesus Christ?

And is there
any real
difference?

childhood
jangle

I hate to
see you go –
I hate to

see you go –
the soundtrack
this moment

battering
my ear – I
hope to hell

you never
come back – vain
wish – vain life –

I hate to
see you go
already.

enuresis

Terror is not – Ed –
sitting in one's piss.
I know – I've sat there –

I've slept there and did
most of my childhood.
That was warmth – in fact –

and comfort – in spite
of the unconcealed
unconcealable

smell. Terror? That was
and always will be
Mother cursing Dad

and there there I am
alone in that night
hearing that door slam.

the
dialogue

What would you like for supper?
My usual answer comes
to dismay her – *Anything.*

and she – as always – tells me
what I know – *That's no answer.*
I eat – of course – what I get.

You may not want to

but you know – as well as I –

this is the limit.

greeting
card

This is the time to

celebrate your being here

with us. Embrace now.

laissez
faire

There's enough
shit in this
world without

our adding
to it – we
admit – but

go right on
happily
shitting it.

Is that the moon

already? What
is it trying

to tell us the

night doesnt far
far more clearly

elucidate?

post
coitum

What we have gotten

into calling – a-
las – reality –

as if that put us

properly in our
place – a little wet

behind the prick yet.

the
fault

What was it you hoped

to get out of this?
What did you think was

really in it for

you? And how could I
have pinpointed you?

Is this my doing?

primeval

Every

one of us
as old now

as the first

one of us
learning still

what's dying.

zzz

What you see is what

you get – believe me. And yet

there's a lot more yet.

the
meaninglessness

We live

because

life wants

us to.

**the
kinks**

We havent worked it
all out yet – of course.
It takes time and it

takes money and it
even takes us. But
you mustnt ask where.

Poetry becomes

that conversation we could

not otherwise have.

my
mistake

Fame? Success? Money?
Power? Property?
Immortality?

Is that what it is
is moving you? I
thought it might be life.

now

This morning

they tell me
I died last

night without

knowing it.
What was that

all about?

We want to

want more than

anything.

Daybreak reminds us –

the hills have arrived just in

time to celebrate.

4

It isnt
what you think
but what you're

thinking: Is
this really
a poem?

for want
...ething to say –
something to tell you –

something you should know –
but to detain you –
keep you from going –

feeling myself here
as long as *you* are –
as long as you *are*.

For whose benefit

are you here? Ask the bug the

tree the sky – yourself.

**the
hungry
ones**

Dont you ever get

sick of eating? Doesnt it

kill you to have to?

**fire
explains**

"Altogether other" – "the

terrible hunger" – the dream
of sleep – to get away with

it – escape. The one death – death

of any one – the nothing
each has been coming to know

knowing what the who you are.

glimpses

If you can

sometimes you
see things as

they are – as

beautiful
as they will

ever get.

Answers every

where you look but no question

anywhere to be found.

summer

A breeze! What

mother – in

her pleasure –

knew as a

miracle!

**o
bon**

Going to

pay respects
to the dead –

as if they

couldve been
forgotten –

rock – flowers.

Did that bird want to

become the mother it is?

Or – more – that egg this?

In the shadow of

a butterfly the echo

of a temple bell.

The goldfish

rest touching

each other.

Harvesting the sun

and earth and sky – who needs

to gild a dragonfly?

Every one makes

a difference but how few

ever care to know.

Look. You are staring
at words on a page –
looking for your life

for the life of them.
What does it mean if
it doesnt mean life?

They're children

They dont know
what they want

They only

know they want
it and they

want it now.

To be or not to...
One hell of a choice.
You want shit for lunch

or a bowl of piss?
But stop complaining.
You got all there is.

Life is re-

membering

and dont you

forget it.

to

Be good enough to

be what you are.

This isnt

getting you
anywhere

but isnt

this where you
were going

gotten you?

Only the living want life
only the dying get it

It takes all the sky there is
to warrant and keep the light

beholden

Suddenly over your eyes
hands blinding binding you – Guess
who! And all at once you know

for the first time it doesnt
matter who but that there are
those hands to be held by there.

Why are you

here? Have you
made up a

good reason?

Or are you
trusting this

to provide?

When America

has made a black wall with all

the names of those of

the Vietnamese who died in

that war life will have grown up.

The father
cuts the wood –
the child's truck
stands waiting.

No matter how
much garbage they
take away more –

it always seems –
remains. Nothing
keeps piling up.

**getting
into
the
jazz**

Living is trite
and death is banal. What
is it all about

if not to amuse
the body for as
long as it's about?

Baseball – fudge – fucking –
music – anything
to wean the mind off

what is happening
and all that isnt.
One and two and three...

You are the divine
presence – all that one
dreams of and dies for

Absolute silence
absolute despair –
a life meaning life.

You are

the rock

shadow.

Life? Dont beg

what you have

yet to give.

5

There's only

one poem:

this is it.

To sit in the room
without a light and
feel the evening come

over the garden
into the house. To
feel it coming home.

Like coming back from

tomorrow and finding it

yesterday. What now?

It's never enough
just to die – or live.
But to live and die

together – at once –
at any moment
every breath give.

It all comes

back to this.

In fact – it

never left.

Stop now and

consider
what it means

not to mean

anything.
Begin to

understand.

Something bothering?

Having to think about it.

It doesnt seem fair.

There's no

surer
way to

get lost

than to
go on

with this.

**so
what**

There is no answer

equal to this – only this

inequality.

headline

A leaf on
the doorstep –
dont even

have to pick
it up to
know the news.

Mountain

go tell

it to

the sky.

It was all

rain until

the sky came.

cicadas

Part of the one sun's

machinery – mechanism –

it seems. It all works.

To find something to

do – to make a do about –

almost convincing.

Music – weaving – computing

getting it all together.

cogwheels

Nothing like

a migraine
to bring out

the blindness

inherent
in trying

to be – what?

136

Entered into it

entertaining attaining

it even as yet.

29

Cling to
release

Breathe slow
breathe long

Breathe gentle
breathe strong

One breath says it all –

all breath is one and the one

forever nothing.

swell

Surge after surge

getting it up
on the shore – the

sand letting it

be – wet by it –
having been had

to become this.

tough
cookie

Chewing rock

tasting dust
getting down

to gristle

bone. Feeling
what it is

to eat air.

Life is excessive –

the rock – without a word – knows –

nothing's monument.

The sun is

family –
the earth grows –

the earth knows –

and the moon
and stars are

memories.

froggy

At any given

moment leaping into the

one eternal splash.

Mountains in mist in

the distance way above and

beyond a street's reach.

It always

comes down and
back to this

but what in

hell this is
remains a

mystery.

n.b.

Life is like
nothing else.
Exactly.

Everything ends

sealed by the approval of

silence perfectly.

A red
thread

on
and at

the no
stage.

Is that
it then?

No. This
is now.

Fukuōji. cɦo.
16 August 1998

index of titles and first lines